Rainbow Stories

1 The Rainbow Forest Story

CHILDREN'S BOOK WITH PARENT'S HANDBOOK

WITH LOVE,
Viera G. Faith

ONCE UPON A TIME

In a forest clearing there lived seven little trees that differed a lot in character. One day three fairies came to the forest. "Did you hear that?" Said a black fairy, "they're fighting about who's most important again. They should be stopped!" So she sent a terrible storm to the trees right away to make them quiet. Darkness set in and the wind howled but the trees fought on. "Stop it!" Said a white fairy, "You see, badness doesn't work. Look, I'll try something. Sun, come and help. I'll tickle them with sunbeams and they'll laugh and hopefully they will understand that by fighting they won't achieve anything." But that didn't help either.

"If badness doesn't work, or goodness neither, we'll try another way," decided the third fairy, a rainbow coloured fairy. She went to the trees one by one and asked them to tell her what they like most about the forest. And when they did this she gave them her magic colours. The trees quietened down and eagerly awaited getting a colour.

"Psst, and you (child's name), watch out! I, the rainbow fairy, have an important job for you. At the end of the story you'll give two fir cones to the tree that you like best," she said.

* The Rainbow Fairy personifies the main principal of RAINBOW NUMBERS & COMMUNICATION ® *(DC&K®)*, which consist of solving and preventing conflicts in relationships.

THE FIRST TREE WAS GIVEN RED

He was overjoyed because red was his favourite colour. He always felt at home in the forest. "Truly, the dew washes me in the morning and after the sun dries me. There's no need to take care of anything, everything works smoothly. If only I didn't have to stand all day on my trunk. It makes me so tired. Hmm, how could I make it better?

"Ah, I've got it! Spiders, come here quickly," and he whispered them his idea. The spiders started working and soon they had a web swinging between two oak trees like a hammock. The tree bounced with joy.

"This is nice. Now anytime I get tired I can take a rest."

And the rainbow fairy said "People are like this too when they are tired. So they simply go for a break to the forest."

THE SECOND TREE WAS GIVEN ORANGE

"Thank you," he said enthusiastically and went over to a mirror. He took another look and frowned: "Look at my needles?! I must get them sorted out quickly and then go on a diet because I think my figure's getting wider." He ran here and there to get everything done in time. He was getting ready for the day when people come to choose the most beautiful trees. Then he squinched his eyes and imagined how he would shine dazzlingly when his twigs will be adorned with beautiful glittering baubles and his needles will be braided with golden confetti.

Suddenly from the mirror sounded a secretive voice:

"What is all this pomposity good for?!" The tree respectfully replied: "If we wrapped beauty up in a present and it gave joy to somebody, then the world would be more and more beautiful. What do you say?"

The rainbow fairy agreed: "Without the beauty of Christmas trees we would hardly leave the familiarity of ordinary days. Because we often forget what is most important in our lives."

THE THIRD TREE FOUND
JOY IN YELLOW

"Wow, I have a sunny colour that I have known since I was little. I'm going for a short walk, so I can get everything under control. Only, who knows if it will rain today. Friends, do you know what the forecast is?"

"Surely it will be nice," croaked a frog from a nearby pond. The tree thought anyway "I will take an umbrella in any case. The frog could be wrong and I'd rather be prepared."

It was almost dark when he came back from his walk and so he quickly stood in a safe place. He was often scared in the night. He was pleased that come the morning everything will be where it belongs, the way he liked it.

Therefore he always felt fearless in the forest and nothing out of place could surprise him.

"Did you notice that people sometimes like to hug trees in the forest? It gives a feeling of security, that they lack so much," said the rainbow fairy.

THE FOURTH TREE WAS GRATEFUL FOR GREEN

"Squirrel, hedgehog, butterfly, come here quick. We've got a green colour and there is enough for everyone. First we'll colour in the twigs on the trees. After we'll paint the bushes and what is left we'll tip on the grass." Finally the forest had a common colour. But when he wanted to colour in the flowers too, the rainbow fairy stopped him:

"Don't overdo it! You've shared enough and also the other trees want to give a bit of their colour to the forest." The tree agreed and so the flowers painted with different colours and red rose hips appeared on the bushes. The all found joy in such beauty. Suddenly out of the bushes came the cry of a little bird which had fallen out of its nest.

"Don't cry little bird, here is your little nest," the tree said gently and with love returned him back. And so it was in the forest every day. Every time somebody needed him, the tree felt he was needed.

Even the rainbow forest fairy felt at home in the forest. The forest is here for everyone and everyone needs the forest. It is a mutual relationship and they cannot live without each other.

THE FIFTH TREE GOT TURQUOISE

With joy he went cycling to a nearby town and on the way back he fell. "It's very busy in the town and there is lots of stress. I had to get out of there. It is time to something beneficial for my body and surely the fresh air will do me good."

He liked the harmony in nature and it filled him up with energy. It is unnecessary to dash somewhere in a hurry with a head full of troubles. He settled in a clearing for arrest, until he fell asleep. He had a beautiful dream where he floated above the forest to the clouds and he felt wonderful. Suddenly in the distance the sound of a car interrupted him. "What an idiot, destroying the forest with the fumes from the car. He completely destroyed my good mood. Never mind, it's time to go home anyway. Tomorrow is another day."

The rainbow fairy feels the same. We can the stress and tension of the people who come to the forest. When they leave the forest they have in their soul peace and energy for the whole week.

THE SIXTH TREE WAS SURPRISED BY BLUE

"What? I've never seen such a colour in the forest," wondered the tree and went off to Google it. Straight away he found out that in the city there are lots of different colours. And his curiosity grew. Although he liked the forest very much he was getting a little bit bored. Suddenly he heard the forest park radio:

"Attention! Trees are required in the city, repeat, trees are required in the city." The blue tree didn't hesitate for a second and went off to pack. However, the animals shouted with alarm: "It's almost dark!"

"It doesn't matter," he replied to them, "I like challenges and the stars will light my way." He was excited about the adventure and new friends. Happily he hopped and in his twigs he felt a wave of new energy.

The rainbow fairy likes to learn too and because of the colours she has learnt lots of new things. The trees quietened down and were now curious what the last colour would bring.

THE SEVENTH TREE
WAS GIVEN PURPLE

The tree wrote down all the new colours. His joy grew when he saw the value the forest had gained. He remembered the day when a magpie flew over the forest and announced some terrible news:

"caw-caw, a strong gale is coming." As he looked around broken twigs were lying on the ground. By the next morning it was a complete catastrophe. He lamented in vain, he had to count everything and find out how it was possible for such a big loss to be straightened up.

He counted that if everyone planted a new tree once a year it would be possible to fix the crisis. He decided that he would find the fairy because she was the one who could go into the world of people to ask for help.

"Your right," answered the rainbow fairy, "I'll do it with pleasure, because everyone manages more when working together with others."

"This story doesn't end like other stories," said the rainbow fairy, "now your assignment (child's name), is to decide which tree in the forest is most important or which one you liked best. You can choose one or two trees. The squirrel will give two fir cones to the tree of your choice. From now on it will be your friend and when you grow up you will find him in the forest. I'm sure you'll recognize him – he will be exactly like you.

On the trees hang bells and that's the end of our story. Now goodnight and sweet dreams!"

* * * * *

For parents: observe your child during the story and try to tell which story they liked best. It probably mirrors their strengths and with this you will know their RAINBOW NUMBER *. This knowledge will be a big support with raising your child. Try not to influence your child's choice of tree.

*The RAINBOW NUMBER is a principle of personal growth on the basis of knowing and developing of personal strengths.

* RAINBOW NUMBERS - The first part of the principle RAINBOW NUMBERS & COMMUNICATION

RAINBOW NUMBERS & COMMUNICATION ®

DEAR PARENTS,

IF YOU ARE AT THE END OF YOUR BREATH

during the upbringing of your children and have to deal with many situations which you are not prepared for, then these words are written just for you. Many times we are not sure if our parenting methods are the right ones. After repeating our methods gradually frustration and hopelessness gets to us and we deal with situations inappropriately. I remember the times when I was hopelessly trying to solve dilemmas during the upbringing of my two daughters, who since being very little, were completely different from one another. Therefore, no matter my reaction, what education techniques worked for one daughter, they didn't work at all with the other one.

We don't learn at school how to raise our children, therefore we naturally try the methods our parents used. But we forget that many things have changed over time and that those techniques are insufficient and don't consider the real needs of our children throughout life.

Perhaps, contrarily, we are trying to raise our children different to how our parents did. Maybe because during childhood, our parents perceived that we weren't prepared enough for our own life, despite their great effort. I personally felt a big difference in having both my parents, because they helped each other with the job of parenting. But my own daughters grew up without their father and it was almost impossible to balance between the feminine and masculine approaches. That is why I have tried different methods, such as studying literature or talking to acquaintances. Doubts of what is right and what is not have followed me most of this beautiful but hard and responsible period up to that moment, when I found the solution, which considerably helped me do deal with these doubts and step by step I brought it in to the raising of my children.

The secret is concealed within the principle of Rainbow Numbers & Communication. It is based on the wisdom of knowing the strengths of yourself and your child, understanding them and using them during upbringing. Rainbow Numbers represent seven categories - DC&K® 1-7 - which characterise those strengths and the different natures of personality, motivation for activities and also three stages, from stagnation through to development up to the dynamic development of personality.

For children aged from three and up, this picture and story format is suitable for a child's perception. Older children are subject to a greater variety of influences and therefore from 12 years old RAINBOW DIAGNOSTICS JUNIOR is more suitable, which you can order at vip@vip-team.eu. It is suitable to choose a high school which would support children in preparation for their future occupation. Often what happens is that parents are trying to realize their unfulfilled dreams and visions of life and are therefore choosing the best school according to their views. The most accurate form of diagnostics for adults can be found on www.rainbownumbers.eu, where you form your rainbow number from 2.8 million options, including combination and intensity DC&K®. The exact knowledge of yourself will open further secrets of your own personal development. DC&K® – the abbreviation for a specific Rainbow Number according to principle of Rainbow Numbers & Communication, which characterizes strengths.

IF YOU ARE LOOKING FOR A SIMPLE ANSWER.

To navigate your child's nature, verify accurately their reactions. So don't waste time and energy with complicated methods. Create a simple system of raising that can support your children in their healthy development, be a role model, teach them better communication and understanding, so you can understand them sufficiently, and therefore you will be a good mother or father to them. The result will be a firm base for their own life, a trouble-free adolescence and good relationships that last a life time.

The first story is about Sam DC&K® 1

One pleasant summer evening we sat with our friends by the fire and frizzled some sausages. Little Sam wanted to grill some too, but the idea that he will have to hold a long stick over a fire discouraged him. He didn't like the fact that he had to put a lot of effort into it, so he walked around thinking how he could solve this. After a while he found a way to fix the stick problem, so he could sit comfortably and have his hands free. During the whole time frizzling, he had a satisfied smile on his face because he managed it make it all easier. ☺

WE GAIN EXCEPTIONAL VALUES

When we define the Rainbow Number for our family members we gradually recognize what is best for us. In everyday life we often see what irritates us in the other person and we want to change it. We see the diversity as a bad thing compared with what is good for us. And yet the diversity end exceptionality of each of us is fundamental. It is evidenced by our unique DNA or our fingertips. Therefore, if during the upbringing we don't change our children, but support them in everything that is important and naturally strong for the child, we will raise a healthy and original person and not a secondary copy.

How we enjoyed a picture from Natalie DC&K® 2

An invitation from the Kindergarten in Orava immensely pleased me.

This book travelled from family to family for almost a year and parents together with their children made a beautiful chronicle in which the children drew their own tree and parents wrote their knowledge and experiences. I couldn't hide the feelings of surprise as they chose the trees according identical to their characteristics. Especially the parents Joseph and Mary, who described the significant behaviour of their daughter. Although in the preperation of this book we took great pains to make the orange tree special enough, it didn´t match up to what Natalie drew. Her tree was completely sparkly, it had added decorations with bold a note "This is all ME" and we couldn't miss her among all the other children. ☺

WE PROVIDE THE CORRECT UPBRINGING OF CHILDREN

We realize that what is good for us doesn't have to be what is good for our child. Therefore understanding the strengths of children is very important. If we try to re-educate them throughout childhood into "our image," in adulthood they will become aware of their own identity and we as parents won't be the support or guarantee of right or wrong. They will start looking for another role model, mostly among their peers, who do not have enough life experience. Hard knocks and their effects ... and we will be able to do absolutely nothing. However if we will prepare them for life, which is given to them characteristically, they will not make unnecessary mistakes, because they will have knowledge of what is good for them and what is not.

My daughter, Victoria DC&K® 3

She is different from me (I am DC&K® 4 and 6) and she has taught me loads in life. Her strength is stability and security, verification of things, a progressive system, and leaves time to make decisions. I on the other hand make decisions quickly, I change things intuitively, I like innovations and look for solutions. If I would be teaching her to live life my way, it would cause an inner chaos and stress, she would often experience setbacks. I made loads of mistakes at first. I remember when we moved, when Victoria completely fell apart, because "I forgot" that she needed to have her time in her room the way she was used to. But gradually I understood what she need and how she was to be internally identified and I supported her in it. She chosefor herself, and according to that she chose a school, later a job and a life partner. For my second daughter Patricia, we had a common DC&K® 4, and that gave us the same outlook on life, understanding of what fulfils us internally. It is important, that we respect our nature and mutually respect these within the family. Today my daughters are grown up and they cause me great delight. ☺

WE CAN SHARE

RAINBOW NUMBERS too with our life partner, with parents, siblings or colleagues at work. The quality of relationships will noticeably improve. I share my personal experience with people in all sorts of projects and the results are indeed extremely interesting. The drawings in this book were created during one of our projects "Plant a Tree, Make a Home" which for the year 2012 created the record number of trees planted in Slovakia. During the creation of the project we used intensively our strengths and today children together with their parents plant each year their trees which benefits the whole world. www.zasadstrom.eu.

The fact that it is necessary to help others is evidenced by DC&K® 4 which is inherited in some of us

Fidgety 4-year-old Gregory did not respond to any commands from his aunt, who cared for him one day. She was at the end of her patience with her commands "Be carefull" or "Don't ride that bike too fast or you are going to get hurt," as if he didn't hear. But then his dad came home and asked his son for help. His reaction was instant. And when he injured his finger during the work he ran to get the first aid and carefully treated him. A mischievous boy turned into an attentive son. How it is possible the aunt wondered? In a family that are familiar with Rainbow Numbers nobody doubts that Gregory "listens" only if he can be useful for somebody. He ignores his own needs and therefore the the commands from his aunt were unimportant. If she would say: "watch out so you wouldn´t hurt anyone if you're riding that fast," then the child would instantly slow down, because he doesn't want to hurt anyone. ☺

FEEL DEEPLY THE HARMONY OF LIFE

If we reduce the level of stress, worries, conflicts we can balance them out with good feelings. It is necessary to start with yourself to find the harmony of body and soul, not to deal with externals, be yourself. From there it is only a small step to a relaxed upbringing. Just do the same as to your children. Instead of remorse for what you didn't do or did wrong, we bring into their lives playfulness and joy. After that we will enjoy the time when raising children enjoy, being together with them and savouring these memorable moments, full of laughter and lightheartedness.

The story of Matt from Kindergarten DC&K® 5 is a good example for teachers:

During one of my visits to a kindergarten, I noticed a small boy, who played alone completely happy at a toy race track. When I drew the teacher's attention to this she quickly explained that this was a troubled boy from another classroom who didn't want to join in to the group. After evaluation his Rainbow Number we found out what his strengths were - not refusing the group as such, but that they would rather join in when they feel like it. So it seemed that they shut themselves up if they were pushed into it. I am glad that the teacher took a lesson from this, and they changed their attitude towards the child and didn't push him anymore. ☺

WE DISCOVER THE RIGHT SOLUTIONS

Whenever we open to new possibilities, which is natural for everyone with DC&K® 6. Do you know why dinosaurs became extinct? Because they could not adapt to change. Therefore as parents, we apprehend the change in the future conditions in which our children will live and we should not cling to the raising methods of our parents, although you can still appreciate them for our upbringing.

As a good example, let us consider leisure time. Sometimes kids spend it outside with friends. In terms of raising, it was therefore natural that parents gave attention to physical security. They did not teach us about Facebook or drugs. Nowadays, when children spend their free time at the computer, we must teach children to face the traps of social networking and various temptations of this period.

In a troubled sixth-grade, in cooperation with psychologists, we tackled the consequences of bullying. Over our trees, we gradually exposed what good was hiding in each of them, how to mutually gel and communicate so that we would not hurt anyone. The result was the self-confidence that children regained. Together, they created a bulletin board called SUPER CLASS, where they visualized all the good that they would like to experience together. They realized that they themselves were responsible for the adventure of life. ☺

CHILDREN ARE OUR WEALTH

They hide inside the value of future life, they enrich our everyday joy, and they are our teachers. They are like little seeds and we have no idea what will grow out of them. That is why we sensitively follow what they need for their life, so we can strengthen their roots and give them wings for their life. We are taking care of them with love and we believe that we give them the best...

 This is a short story of a known writer which tries to explain what money is for in life. While listening to a daughter talking to son, "I have got so much money that I could buy the whole world." Little George answered calmly, "but I won't sell it to you." ☺

Only children with DC&K® 7 are best able to compare these values.

Another example is 3 year old Mark, who bitterly demanded some candy. We wanted him to wait until the clock showed three, and strangely he calmed down and obediently waited. Exactly a quarter of an hour later he came and asked for three candies. ☺

These were only a few stories about how we can clearly recognize the strengths of our children. And now let's look together at what is hidden in your child using their DC&K®.

With Love,

Viera G. Faith

Choose your favourite picture and according to the number on the left side see how a child would perceive various situations through your eyes. On the right side locate your child's number (numbers and colour maximum up to two trees to which he/she allocated acorns). Rainbow numbers are often in combinations of two, so it does not matter whether your child chose one or two trees. He/ she cannot choose more options. From what you read, try to understand your child's personality and strengths that are important in its development. Accept it during upbringing and in resolving conflicts. The same numbers give greater assumption of consistency; the differences are opportunities for your mutual development.

With this playful form you can obtain a result, which may be subject to momentary influence at the child. With the careful reading of profiles for all DC&K°, which are located in the second part of the book, you can clearly define the strengths of the child. With further returning to the individual tales you can expand and test your knowledge

NUMBERS FOR PARENTS

Cut here --

NUMBERS FOR CHILDREN

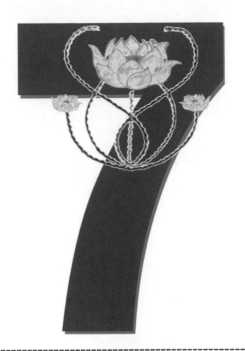

Cut here ---

32

Rainbow number DC&K® 7

Your child has acquired effective thinking for life, therefore give them plenty of facts and quantifiable information which they are able to evaluate.

At school you can motivate them to achieve good grades with suitable pocket money, give them exact numerical instructions, define time limits or set number of tasks which they have to do and negotiate better conditions, for example.

Ineffective sequence of tasks without positive results, where they have to give more than they get back, will make them evaluate and speculative. They would rather wait for more preferable conditions.

Cut here --

Rainbow number DC&K® 1

Your child has been given simplicity of thought, lightness, and a carefree attitude, therefore help them with different tools that make their life easier.

For example, learning with the help of a list, which would bring together the core of a curriculum, making tasks easier by breaking them down. Step by step instructions make learning not so hard. Offer adequate help and try to avoid difficult situations by making satisfactory preparation.

Pressures, conflicts and difficulties get a child into stagnation and therefore this sometimes appears as laziness and without interest.

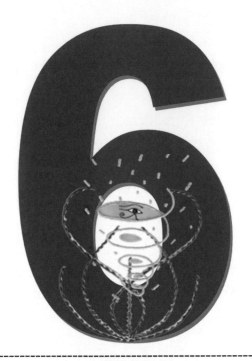

Cut here --

Rainbow number DC&K® 6

Your child lives in a creative world and always follows something new. Therefore give them freedom and space for change and adventure.

The more colourful there is the more energetic they are. They are able to do a thousand things at a time and they love change. Give them surprises, explore the world with them and share secrets with them. Mind that they have their freedom and room for independence.

Boredom and consistency will stifle them and they often don't finish things. They are like the wind which is naturally erratic, therefore do not on the events of yesterday. Today everything can be different.

Cut here --

Rainbow number DC&K® 2

You have an exceptional child, who in life wants to achieve more than others, and therefore motivate them so they will transform their efforts into the best possible results. Observe their achievements and praise them well. Expect better results from school, pay attention to how they dress and support them in their efforts to excel. Involve them in activities where they demonstrate their talents. Gradually raise expectations.

Lecture them one-to-one otherwise they will let you see their offended ego. If unsuccessful, which may be taken badly then they will not ask for help, but they need to feel that they are believed and supported.

Cut here ---

Rainbow number DC&K® 5

Your child is driven by feelings and senses the harmony of life. Therefore allow them to enjoy everything good that life brings and provide a healthy life for them.

They really enjoy a carefree life and therefore they take every difficult situation easily. For harmony in their life, balance school and homework with sport and fun. Grant them all that is good for their body and soul in the right amounts taking into account their responsibilities.

If you require something from them, beyond their willingness, they will clearly let you know their resentment. Whatever bad feeling they have can cause stagnation.

Cut here ---

Rainbow number DC&K® 3

Certainty and security in life is what your child needs. Therefore provide stable and secure environment.

Your child can manage to fulfil tasks systematically and regularly. Therefore you need to allow adequate time for preparation. Together make a schedule and allow the child utilize and manage this system. The child often needs advice from multiple sources so they choose their best result. Allow them time to think things through.

Watch out for stress, risk or sudden changes. Often they succumb to fear, if so watch out for inactive behaviour.

Cut here ---

Rainbow number DC&K® 4

The meaning of your child's life is to be of use to others. Therefore share love and help with them which they will spread out.

Support their activities and good deeds, connect them to group sports or activities so they will never be alone. Teach them to give a 50:50 proportion, thanks to which help will be more effective. Emphasize often that they are needed and that what they do has purpose for their classroom, friends, and family.

If they have the feeling they are not useful they will lose enthusiasm to do things. Their good nature might be taken advantage of almost every time they overdo their share of giving 100:0.

Cut here --

Rainbow number DC&K® 4

The meaning of your child's life is to be of use to others. Therefore share love and help with them which they will spread out.

Support their activities and good deeds, connect them to group sports or activities so they will never be alone. Teach them to give a 50:50 proportion, thanks to which help will be more effective. Emphasize often that they are needed and that what they do has purpose for their classroom, friends, and family.

If they have the feeling they are not useful they will lose enthusiasm to do things. Their good nature might be taken advantage of almost every time they overdo their share of giving 100:0.

Cut here ---

40

Rainbow number DC&K® 3

Certainty and security in life is what your child needs. Therefore provide stable and secure environment.

Your child can manage to fulfil tasks systematically and regularly. Therefore you need to allow adequate time for preparation. Together make a schedule and allow the child utilize and manage this system. The child often needs advice from multiple sources so they choose their best result. Allow them time to think things through.

Watch out for stress, risk or sudden changes. Often they succumb to fear, if so watch out for inactive behaviour.

Cut here --

Rainbow number DC&K® 5

Your child is driven by feelings and senses the harmony of life. Therefore allow them to enjoy everything good that life brings and provide a healthy life for them.

They really enjoy a carefree life and therefore they take every difficult situation easily. For harmony in their life, balance school and homework with sport and fun. Grant them all that is good for their body and soul in the right amounts taking into account their responsibilities.

If you require something from them, beyond their willingness, they will clearly let you know their resentment. Whatever bad feeling they have can cause stagnation.

Cut here --

Rainbow number DC&K® 2

You have an exceptional child, who in life wants to achieve more than others, and therefore motivate them so they will transform their efforts into the best possible results. Observe their achievements and praise them well. Expect better results from school, pay attention to how they dress and support them in their efforts to excel. Involve them in activities where they demonstrate their talents. Gradually raise expectations.

Lecture them one-to-one otherwise they will let you see their offended ego. If unsuccessful, which may be taken badly then they will not ask for help, but they need to feel that they are believed and supported.

Cut here ---

Rainbow number DC&K® 6

Your child lives in a creative world and always follows something new. Therefore give them freedom and space for change and adventure.

The more colourful there is the more energetic they are. They are able to do a thousand things at a time and they love change. Give them surprises, explore the world with them and share secrets with them. Mind that they have their freedom and room for independence.

Boredom and consistency will stifle them and they often don't finish things. They are like the wind which is naturally erratic, therefore do not on the events of yesterday. Today everything can be different.

Cut here --

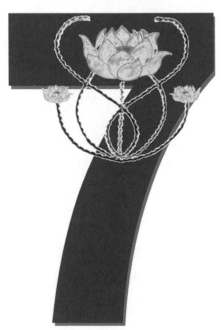

44

Rainbow number DC&K® 1

Your child has been given simplicity of thought, lightness, and a carefree attitude, therefore help them with different tools that make their life easier.

For example, learning with the help of a list, which would bring together the core of a curriculum, making tasks easier by breaking them down. Step by step instructions make learning not so hard. Offer adequate help and try to avoid difficult situations by making satisfactory preparation.

Pressures, conflicts and difficulties get a child into stagnation and therefore this sometimes appears as laziness and without interest.

Cut here --

Rainbow number DC&K® 7

Your child has acquired effective thinking for life, therefore give them plenty of facts and quantifiable information which they are able to evaluate.

At school you can motivate them to achieve good grades with suitable pocket money, give them exact numerical instructions, define time limits or set number of tasks which they have to do and negotiate better conditions, for example.

Ineffective sequence of tasks without positive results, where they have to give more than they get back, will make them evaluate and speculative. They would rather wait for more preferable conditions.

www.vip-team.eu

www.tajch.eu

www.rainbownumbers.eu

www.babytrees.sk

Thank you

To my mum, daughters, partner, siblings, colleagues, friends, and children are everything and I thank them very much. It pleases me that together with you I can bring the knowledge of RAINBOW NUMBERS & COMMUNICATION ® into working projects, homes and also into children's upbringings. I believe this contributes to the understanding of interpersonal relationships and shows the true beauty that is hidden inside all of us.

Thanks to my teachers for big inspiration and knowledge.

With love,
Viera G. Faith

ABOUT THE AUTHOR

I was born in a small village called Ľutina in Slovakia.

The Principal RAINBOW NUMBERS & COMMUNICATION ®, *I have applied in practice for more than eleven years and* the knowledge of learning about people my whole life. It has helped me with my two daughters who I raised alone and it was a truely valuable help.

In the sphere of work, I fulfiled my top ambitions in my career, and I have carried over these principles into projects such as PLANT A TREE, MAKE A HOME, SOS Angel and DC&K® ACADEMY.

They have played a truly important role in finding my true love and thus they fulfilled even my secretest desires. I live my life the way I feel inside my heart and I am extremely grateful to my DC&K® 4466 that conceals a desire to discover and share.

Today I want to share the principle of RAINBOW NUMBERS & COMMUNICATION ® with you. I believe that exploring the knowledge of the strengths will bring you to the true values of life, you will learn to understand and share the joy of life, it will acknowledge your intuitive feelings, show you a simple solutions to a life filled with love and understanding.

With Love Viera G. Faith

Balboa Press books may be ordered through booksellers or by contacting:

Balboa Press
A Division of Hay House
1663 Liberty Drive
Bloomington, IN 47403
www.balboapress.com
1 (877) 407-4847

ISBN:978-1-5043-3820-2 (sc)
ISBN: 978-1-5043-3821-9 (e)

Print information available on the last page.

Balboa Press rev. date: 11/30/2015

BALBOA
PRESS
A DIVISION OF HAY HOUSE

Printed in the United States
By Bookmasters